BEASTLY BOOKS FOR THE BRAVE

THIS BOOK HAS TEETH!

THERESA EMMINIZER

Please visit our website, www.garethstevens.com. For a free color catalog of all our high-quality books, call toll free 1-800-542-2595 or fax 1-877-542-2596.

Cataloging-in-Publication Data

Names: Emminizer, Theresa.
Title: This book has teeth! / Theresa Emminizer.
Description: New York : Gareth Stevens Publishing, 2020. | Series: Beastly books for the brave | Includes glossary and index.
Identifiers: ISBN 9781538233597 (pbk.) | ISBN 9781538233610 (library bound) | ISBN 9781538233603 (6pack)
Subjects: LCSH: Teeth--Juvenile literature. | Bites and stings--Juvenile literature. | Animals--Food--Juvenile literature. | Predatory animals--Juvenile literature.
Classification: LCC QL858.E46 2020 | DDC 591.47--dc23

First Edition

Published in 2020 by
Gareth Stevens Publishing
111 East 14th Street, Suite 349
New York, NY 10003

Designer: Katelyn E. Reynolds
Editor: Kate Light

Photo credits: Cover, p. 1 (teeth) Mogens Trolle/Shutterstock.com; cover, pp. 1-24 (book cover) Ensuper/Shutterstock.com; cover, p. 1-24 (tape) Picsfive/Shutterstock.com; cover, pp. 1-24 (decorative elements) cute vector art/Shutterstock.com; cover, pp. 1-24 (book interior and wood background) robert_s/Shutterstock.com; p. 4-21 (fun fact background) Miloje/Shutterstock.com; p. 5 1lyallmllayllp/Shutterstock.com; pp. 7, 21 (great white shark) Alessandro De Maddalena/ Shutterstock.com; pp. 9, 21 (hippo) Johan Swanepoel/Shutterstock.com; pp. 11 (main), 21 (piranha) Fabian Schmiedlechner/EyeEm/Getty Images; p. 11 (inset) Ondrej Prosicky/Shutterstock.com; pp. 13, 21 (jaguar) ben landy/Shutterstock.com; p. 15 (both) Joe McDonald/Corbis Documentary/Getty Images; p. 17 Procy/Shutterstock.com; p. 18 FiledIMAGE/Shutterstock.com; pp. 19, 21 (saltwater crocodile) PomInOz/Shutterstock.com; p. 21 (human) Beetroot Studio/Shutterstock.com.

Printed in the United States of America

CPSIA compliance information: Batch #CS19GS: For further information contact Gareth Stevens, New York, New York at 1-800-542-2595.

CONTENTS

Words in the glossary appear in **bold** type the first time they are used in the text.

CHECK OUT THOSE CHOMPERS!

Teeth are some of nature's greatest tools and weapons! From **ferocious** fish to horrifying hippos, many animals rely on their teeth to survive. Whether they're cutting through flesh, **injecting** venom, or clashing in a battle for **dominance**, a set of superstrong teeth can mean the difference between life and death.

Teeth can teach you a lot about an animal, but you'll have to take a closer look. Prepare to peek into the mouths of some of the scariest animals on Earth. But be careful, they bite!

FACTS FOR THE FEARLESS

VENOM IS SOMETHING AN ANIMAL MAKES IN ITS BODY THAT CAN HARM OTHER ANIMALS. IT'S COMMONLY DELIVERED THROUGH AN ANIMAL'S TEETH!

Some long-tailed macaques, like the one pictured here, clean their teeth by flossing with human hair!

JAGGED JAWS

What creature has up to 300 teeth but doesn't chew its food? The great white shark! Instead of chewing, they rip their food into pieces and swallow the chunks whole.

Great white shark teeth are arranged in rows. The teeth in the lower jaw are used to **pierce** the shark's prey. The teeth in the upper jaw are used to saw it into pieces. Each row of the upper jaw has 26 teeth, and each row of the lower jaw has 24 teeth.

FACTS FOR THE FEARLESS

HUMANS SOMETIMES HUNT GREAT WHITE SHARKS FOR THEIR TEETH AND JAWS, WHICH ARE SOLD AS PRIZES. BECAUSE OF THIS AND OTHER PROBLEMS, GREAT WHITE SHARK POPULATIONS ARE IN DANGER.

Shark teeth are triangle-shaped and **serrated.** They fall out and are replaced throughout the shark's life.

TERRIFYING TUSKS

Hippopotamuses are herbivores, or plant eaters. So why do they need such big, scary teeth? Hippos use their teeth for more than eating!

One big male leads a group of hippos. Male hippos fight each other for territories and **mates**. They fight with the long teeth in their lower jaw, called tusks. Male hippos open their mouths wide in a "yawn" to show off their tusks and scare away other males. If this doesn't work, they will use their tusks to fight.

FACTS FOR THE FEARLESS

HIPPOPOTAMUS TUSKS CAN GROW MORE THAN 1 FOOT (0.3 M) LONG! THEY'RE SHARP ENOUGH TO CUT THROUGH A HIPPO'S THICK HIDE, OR SKIN.

Hippos are some of the most dangerous animals in Africa. They're very **aggressive** and have been known to attack people.

A MIGHTY BITE

In the Tupí language spoken by the native people of Brazil, "piranha" means "tooth fish." There are more than 30 species of piranha living in the lakes and rivers of South America. Some are even vegetarians, which means they don't eat meat! Meat-eating piranhas have sharp, triangular teeth that are serrated.

The black piranha has the strongest recorded bite of any fish. Their powerful jaws make up 2 percent of their body weight! But although they are famously fierce, piranhas don't usually attack people.

FACTS FOR THE FEARLESS

DID YOU KNOW THAT PIRANHAS BARK? RED-BELLIED PIRANHAS MAKE A GRUNTING, BARK-LIKE SOUND TO WARN AWAY OTHER FISH.

Meat-eating piranhas have sharp teeth that cut like scissors. Plant-eating piranhas have flat teeth that look similar to ours!

KILLER CATS

You made it past the piranhas in one piece! But another fearsome predator is on the hunt—the deadly jaguar. It can kill in a single bite!

Jaguars have a special way of killing their prey. Most big cats attack their prey's throat, but jaguars go for the head. A jaguar's bite is so powerful that its teeth pierce through the prey's skull and into its brain. With its strong jaws and teeth, a jaguar can even bite through turtle shells!

FACTS FOR THE FEARLESS

JAGUARS HUNT ALMOST ANYTHING THEY CAN FIND, INCLUDING DEER, SNAKES, AND EVEN CROCODILES. THEY SOMETIMES CLIMB TREES AND AMBUSH, OR SURPRISE ATTACK, THEIR PREY FROM ABOVE.

Jaguars are the biggest cats in the Americas. They're the third largest felines in the world, after the tiger and lion.

FRIGHTENING FANGS

Rattlesnakes have special fangs that they use to inject venom into their prey. Venomous fangs are hollow. They're attached to venom **glands** at the base of the jaw. When the snake sinks its fangs into an animal, the venom flows through the fangs into the prey.

How do rattlesnakes manage not to stab themselves with their fangs? Their fangs are foldable! Rattlesnake fangs are attached to the jaw by a **hinge**, so they fold up when the snake's mouth is closed.

FACTS FOR THE FEARLESS

SOMETIMES RATTLESNAKES LOSE THEIR FANGS. BEHIND EACH FANG, THERE ARE SEVEN GROWING FANGS TO REPLACE IT. RATTLESNAKE FANGS CAN GROW UP TO 6 INCHES (15 CM) LONG!

VENOM DRIPPING FROM A FANG

MEASURING UP TO 7 FEET (2.1 M) LONG, EASTERN DIAMONDBACK RATTLESNAKES ARE THE BIGGEST VENOMOUS SNAKES IN NORTH AMERICA.

TOUGH TEETH

Teeth aren't just for attacking and defending. They're also for building! Beavers use their supertough teeth to cut down trees to build dams.

Beaver teeth are self-sharpening. The back side of a beaver's tooth is softer than the **enamel** that coats the front side. Because of this, the back side wears away faster than the enamel, creating a sharp edge. Beavers' large front teeth, or incisors, never stop growing. They keep them from getting too long by gnawing, or chewing, on trees.

FACTS FOR THE FEARLESS

Beavers have orange teeth! That's because there's iron in the enamel of their teeth. This enamel keeps the teeth from **decaying**.

Beavers' incisors grow at a rate of almost 0.2 inch (0.5 cm) a month!

SCARY SMILES

Would you be brave enough to smile at a crocodile? Their mouths are filled with more than 60 deadly teeth, some of which are over 4 inches (10.1 cm) long!

Saltwater crocodiles are huge. Some weigh up to 2,200 pounds (997.9 kg) and can be 23 feet (7 m) long. Although they can swim very fast, crocodiles don't usually chase their prey. They like surprise attacks, using their long jaws that are specially designed to grab and hold onto prey.

You can see a crocodile's teeth even when its mouth is closed!

If a crocodile loses a tooth, it's able to grow a new one to replace it!

WHICH WEAPONS WIN?

You survived all the biting beasts in this book! Which teeth were the most terrifying? The great white shark had the most teeth, but the hippopotamus had the longest tusks. The jaguar killed in a single bite, but the rattlesnake injected venom with its fangs!

One way to measure the power of teeth is to look at bite force. Scientists haven't tested every animal for bite force yet. Look at these ranked bite forces to decide which bite is the scariest!

Bite Force Ranked

PIRANHA

72 PSI

HUMAN

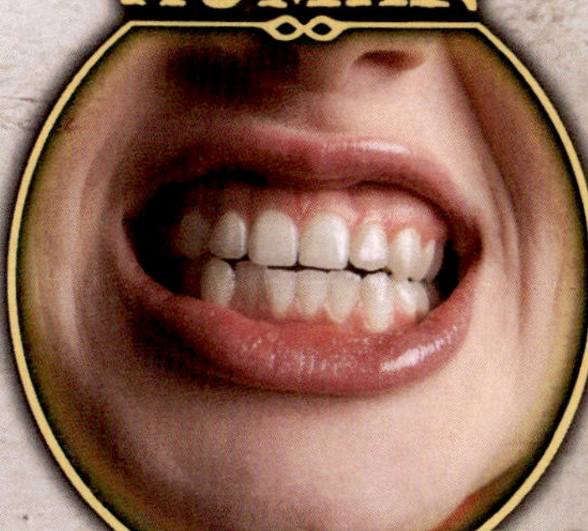

200 PSI

JAGUAR

1,500 PSI

HIPPO

1,800 PSI

SALTWATER CROCODILE

3,700 PSI

GREAT WHITE SHARK

4,000 PSI

PSI = Pounds Per Square Inch

The PSI of the great white shark was an **estimate** made in a lab. The saltwater crocodile has the most powerful recorded bite of a living animal.

GLOSSARY

aggressive: acting with forceful energy and determination. Also, showing a readiness to attack.

decay: to break down over time

dominance: power or control over something

enamel: a protective coating on teeth

estimate: a careful guess about an answer based on the known facts

ferocious: fierce and wild

gland: a body part that produces something needed for a bodily function

hinge: a movable joint on which a part swings

inject: to use sharp teeth to force venom into an animal's body

mate: one of two animals that come together to make babies

pierce: to make a hole through

serrated: having a jagged edge

For More Information

BOOKS

Cargill-Greer, Stephanie. *Fighting With Fangs and Claws.* New York, NY: PowerKids Press, 2018.

Markle, Sandra, and Howard McWilliam. *What If You Had Animal Teeth?.* New York, NY: Scholastic Inc, 2013.

Polydoros, Lori. *Piranhas: On the Hunt.* North Mankato, MN: Capstone Press, 2016.

WEBSITES

Red-Bellied Piranha
kids.nationalgeographic.com/animals/red-bellied-piranha/#red-bellied-piranha-bellies.jpg
For more facts about these feisty fish, go to this fun site!

San Diego Zoo - Kids
kids.sandiegozoo.org/
Learn about different animal species, their habits, and adaptations at this interactive site.

Types of Teeth
www.dkfindout.com/us/animals-and-nature/food-chains/types-teeth/
Learn the difference between teeth used for eating plants and teeth used for eating meat here!

INDEX